I THRIVE
iN
LOVE

AG

EVERYDAY MAGNIFICENT

PRACTICES TO ACTIVATE AN UNLIMITED LIFE

BALBOA.
PRESS

A DIVISION OF HAY HOUSE

Balboa Press books may be ordered through booksellers or by contacting:

Balboa Press
A Division of Hay House
1663 Liberty Drive
Bloomington, IN 47403
www.balboapress.com
1 (877) 407-4847

Because of the dynamic nature of the Internet, any web addresses or links contained in this book may have changed since publication and may no longer be valid. The views expressed in this work are solely those of the author and do not necessarily reflect the views of the publisher, and the publisher hereby disclaims any responsibility for them.

The author of this book does not dispense medical advice or prescribe the use of any technique as a form of treatment for physical, emotional, or medical problems without the advice of a physician, either directly or indirectly. The intent of the author is only to offer information of a general nature to help you in your quest for emotional and spiritual well-being. In the event you use any of the information in this book for yourself, which is your constitutional right, the author and the publisher assume no responsibility for your actions.

Any people depicted in stock imagery provided by Getty Images are models, and such images are being used for illustrative purposes only.
Certain stock imagery © Getty Images.

ISBN:978-1-5043-9885-5 (sc)
ISBN: 978-1-5043-9886-2 (e)

Library of Congress Control Number: 2018904276

This book is a work of non-fiction. Unless otherwise noted, the author and the publisher make no explicit guarantees as to the accuracy of the information contained in this book and in some cases, names of people and places have been altered to protect their privacy.

Print information available on the last page.

Balboa Press rev. date: 04/25/2018

Contents

Suggested Supplies

- Colors! (pencils, pens, crayons, pastels, etc.)
- Collage images
- Scissors
- Glue or double stick tape
- Willing, playful, uncensored expression
- An earnest heart

Acknowledgments

I acknowledge the Mystery and offer gratitude for the generosity of energy so freely given to us all. No matter the territory I traverse, in many dimensions, I continue to be blown away by the love and magnificence of the One orchestrating it all. I acknowledge this creative force, first and foremost, in all infinite forms and formlessness, seen and unseen. Its vast beauty, benevolence, guidance, and patience is beyond measure. The wisdom, resources, opportunities, and bounty of gifts we are given are unlimited. THANK YOU!

I am grateful for the planet Earth and acknowledge the natural world, elementals and wild ones who are models of the sacred patterning of Creation. I acknowledge the human experience as a vehicle for awakening.

I bow to all whom share the journey as we learn forward into being love and living by Quantum laws. I give thanks for the many mentors and guides along the way. I offer gratitude to Dr. Joe Dispenza, for marrying mysticism and science with brilliant articulation and life application. This book was birthed in his trainings, as my way to process and integrate the geyser of energy rising within me. It evolved into these practices to deepen the conversation with the Divine, and sustain embodiment of our unlimited nature.

I acknowledge and give thanks to my beloved family, soul companions and to the hundreds of willing participants who experimented with this journal in pilot programs. I offer heart full gratitude to my steady, daily life partners, Kenya Solomon and Talia Masala, who walked every step of this process beside me. Divine ones, you are Everyday Magnificent.

Ubuntu...I am because We All Are.

Introduction

This journal is a portal. Step through and enjoy the mystical, practical journey into your unlimited nature and into an unlimited life. We'll be playing in the Quantum, the mysterious Unified Field of information and energy, where all potentials exist in the present moment. We are going beyond predictable definitions of ourselves and reality. We will be practicing to empty out conditioned programs, clear out old habituated ways of feeling, being and doing. We will step out of our own way, allowing our unlimited nature to activate and drive our lives.

The words Quantum, Unified Field, Creator, Source, The Divine, The Unknown and Mystery are used interchangeably. Replace them with God, Goddess, Great Spirit or any devotional or scientific name that resonates more for you. Cultivating deeper intimacy with this unified force, as our creative source and unlimited nature, is what we are up to in this journal. Give this force attention, expression, love and gratitude (inside and out).

Make a practice of offering yourself to the Unknown, for the duration of this journey. Experiment with surrendering into this current and letting it carry you. Befriend it. Trust it. Let it steer and guide your life. Let's allow the Quantum to help us remember who we really are. What we really are... vast, unlimited energy. Miraculous. Magnificent.

This workbook is for those curious to dive into an adventure of creativity, deep play, freedom and communion with the Divine. Willing effort, presence and surrender is essential.

This journal is an incubator and pollinator for all that expresses, creates and lives through you. Give yourself a season and use your journal daily. Engage earnestly with the activities, practices and touchstones. Let the process light you up from the inside out.

Living magnificently is not a predictable science. It is an art. Explore the art of your life design, and enjoy the mystical experiment of conscious co-creation with your unlimited nature, as it gives rise to an embodied, unlimited life of love.

How to Use This Book

This journal is a companion guide to your life adventure. The contemplative activities, practices, and touchstones are tools to structure your transformational journey through a field of infinite possibilities. Engage in the process and observe as your daily life expands with increased awareness, authenticity and aliveness.

Use the process to cultivate a living state of gratitude and wholeness. It will serve to nourish a magnificent, unlimited life. Use the journey to build trust in turning directly to Source energy, the Unified Field - within you and all around you - as your creative companion and loving collaborator.

Fill these pages with color, images, energy sketches and words of wisdom. Be playful and savor your exploration with your unlimited nature; your creative intelligence, intuition and infinite potential. Embody your joy and genius!

Respond to the prompts in full sensory detail. Savor them as you might a delicious meal. Write in detail activating your vision, sense of touch, sight, sound and feeling awareness. Engage your imagination and the intelligence of your whole brain to make the responses real, before they manifest. Detail how you will move, behave, feel and what you will experience as you live into your inquiry responses.

These are not meditations or creativity practices to catch a high, or positively think your way into a better version of an old world view. These practices, along with the whole process are designed for the whole heart, brain and body to flow in a symphony of co-creative partnership with the unseen, unlimited power of life. We are entering into multiple and inter-dimensional reality; experimenting with grounding new possibilities from the field of energy potentials into the manifest realm. For more detailed information, research and resources on these perspectives, (including mental rehearsal, meditation, spontaneous healing and manifestation) please visit www.drjoedispenza.com.

Follow these simple guidelines to get the most out of your Everyday Magnificent experience.

Start by reading the outline of journal tools and practices. Familiarize yourself with the activities, practices and touchstones. Refer back to the outline as needed as you fill out a new journal page.

Apply yourself wholeheartedly, and this process will offer you a contemplative reflection of your evolutionary edge. Commit to daily practice and a season of transformation. Take ninety days to complete this journal. Receive three months to flower into an embodied experience of *Everyday Magnificent.*

Show up to your journal as you would a date with a best friend or a divine appointment with destiny. Integrate it into your morning and/or evening routines. Bring it along with you as a companion field journal to your life. Explore your unlimited nature and deepen relationship with the infinite and unseen dimensions of being. **Allow repetition of the activities, practices and touchstones to build momentum.**

Invite the Mystery to speak uniquely to you, unhindered and uncensored. Play with un-knowing and un-learning. Give voice and image to the unseen. Go beyond the analytical mind and be free. *Improvise!* **This is a love affair, a communion with your life force.** Get into it! If you meet resistance, don't recoil. Unfold deeper into the Unknown. Engage. Embody. Surrender.

Drop Judgment. It is our birth right to express creativity. We are all life artists in our unique way. Kindly drop ideas of *product* art and simply allow creative process art to flow.

While this is a self paced experiment, you will receive the best results if you journal daily and integrate the process into life. Reference, review and do the practices and touchstones as well as filling the journal page. Together, in concert with the foundational activities this will ignite an atmosphere of new possibilities in your life.
- Use a practice and Journal page as a daily meditation
- Journal in the morning to set the tone of your day and review it before bedtime
- Journal daily: follow page prompts, use the touchstone and engage activities and practices
- Use it solo, and/or share the tools with friends, family, community.

Some of the practices offered will invite you to elevate your state. Don't try to force this. Instead, find the flow by playfully matching the feeling frequency of your desired state. Each state already exists as a potential in the Quantum Field. Use the practices offered with intention and purpose to tune into the frequency, then bridge and live it into daily life. Note: This is not a dualistic approach focusing only on positivity. We are embracing our journey, creating from wholeness without negating our life or experience. We are experimenting with cocreative manifestation and living by Quantum laws. We are changing our worldview from a paradigm of lack and separation, to a paradigm, of unity.

Reread and revisit these guidelines. Intentionally fill these pages with wisdom, passion and unique guidance from the Field. The activities, practices and touchstones are repetitious and random on purpose. They may stir up a little chaos. Welcome this as a precursor to transformation. We are building infrastructure for our Quantum leaps. Go beyond resistance into phenomenal shifts. We are the mystics, reality artists and alchemists at the heart of it all. Trust intuition and fall in love with this magnificent life adventure.

Everyday Magnificent
Outline of Tools and Practices

Foundational Activities

Journaling

Journaling is a contemplative meditation tool. It accesses the authentic voice, and reveals gems of awareness to enrich our lives. We suggest you practice "sprint" journaling, for all the writing exercises. Sprint journaling means writing in a continuous stream of consciousness, without much "thinking." Hold the intention to deepen beyond superficial content and move beyond the voice of the inner critic and censor. We encourage being spontaneous, playful and vulnerable in your writing responses. Surprise yourself with what emerges rather than habituating to the conditioned response. Allow your responses to access the mind of the universe and intelligence of your unlimited nature. Animate your words, and detail your feeling state with full sensory descriptions. Use the power of words to harmonize, create from wholeness, appreciate life and spark new possibilities.

Free Write Prompts and Inquiry

Before responding to the prompts and inquiries, take a moment to center within and quiet your mind. You may choose to practice a meditation or touchstone first. Respond with the same quality of presence and attention you would give a beloved friend. Take focused time to complete your responses authentically without censorship. Invite your unlimited nature to guide the way. Inquiry and open ended sentence stems have a way of tapping us into the infinite field of possibilities where all potentials exist simultaneously. As we respond in sensory detail, we are matching our vibrational frequency to the potential that already exists in the field. This creates an electromagnetic signature that calls the potential into activation and manifestation.

Gratitude and Synchronicity

Focus your attention on all which generates gratitude and reminds you of magnificence in your life. List and detail where you are experiencing gratitude, and perceiving synchronicities. Notate specific ways you are feeling grateful, seeing interconnection and alignment with the Unified Field. These moments may have a whimsical sense of being tickled, awed or surprised by life. They may even have a quality of the miraculous, appearing "out of nowhere". Gratitude is a fast track to flowing with our unlimited nature. Learn to look for it, see it, appreciate it and flood it through your field of awareness.

Source Creations

What are you called to bring into manifestation? This tool helps to detail the life you are inspired to create. Include both short term and long-range creations that are informed by your Source, and call you to be and give your best. These likely point towards dreams, visions and expressions of your soul evolution, passion, joy and contribution to the whole of life.

Empowered Actions

Empowered Actions are those you can integrate immediately as you move into your day or week. Actions can be tasks as well as behavioral practices, that shift habits and develop new skills. Marry intention with effort and follow through by living these into action in your daily life.

To BE Lists

Invite deeper, more intentional Being in all you are doing. How do you want to feel? What states do you want to experience and what do you want to emanate? How will you show up to the Being of your doing, of your living? List it!

To BE Today:
- *Happy/Joyful from the inside out*
- *Patient*
- *Magnificent*
- *Whole*
- *Integrated/Balanced*
- *LOVE*
- *Vibrant*
- *Energized*
- *Honest*
- *Affectionate*

Distillations

Every 10-20 pages of your Journal, you will find a Distillation. After a meditation practice or touchstone of your choice, reread the content from past Journal entries to distill essential wisdom. As you reflect on your writing and drawings, use a different colored marker or pen to underline, highlight or circle repetitive words and phrases that "pop" out at you. Pay attention to words with an energized presence for you.

Be intuitive and concise as you are guided to the words and phrases which best distill a core message from your inner-most self. Next, on the Distillation journal page, write only the highlighted, underlined, circled words in the sequential order they appeared. Consider this a summary of loving intelligence, from the Quantum Field, emerging especially for you. Free write any additional reflections or awareness. Once complete, read it out loud. Listen for affirmative direction and guidance offered back to you.

Open Reflection

There are pages left blank intentionally. They are meant for reflection. Use them as inspired to journal, create energy sketches, images or symbols from your inner journey.

Mandalas

Mandala is a Sanskrit word meaning sacred circle. Found in virtually every culture, mandalas are utilized for meditative purposes, healing rituals and ceremonies. Their circular form reflects the harmony of nature and containment of the whole. Creating within a circle, offers an avenue for the unconscious to express and unify with daily life matters. It's an evolutionary form of "process art" that shifts awareness, reveals insights and creates whole being coherence. Drawing elevates states, creating the chemistry of connection and relaxation. Creating mandalas, taps whole brain intelligence and integration. It offers access to information beyond linear, written language, to the language of the soul.

Mandala pages include single, series (for an evolutionary reflection), and Dream Design templates. **Single Mandalas** capture the wholeness of a moment, area of inquiry or reflection from the nonverbal realms. **The Mandala Series** can be used to receive insight, digest a process or discover more information about any area of inquiry through a progression. Begin with issue or subject of awareness in first mandala. In the second mandala, invite transformational guidance into the process. Complete the final mandala with receptivity of resolve, and gratitude for answered prayers. Notice the shift in your state as well as what the progression of color and energy has revealed.

As you explore with your mandalas, use color, images, or symbols and unleash creative inspiration. Allow "energy" sketches to emerge, rather than being bound by mental images or preconceived ideas of what to draw. You can choose to draw with (or without) a specific focus or inquiry. Create a mandala after meditation to ground awareness, or use the content of your writing prompts and life journey. As always, invite your unlimited nature to express through you.

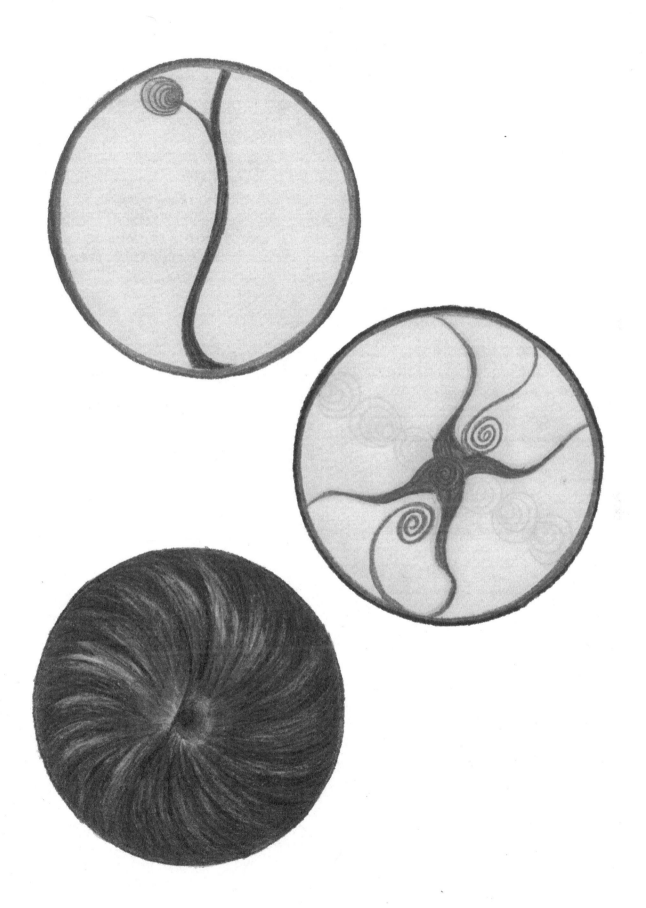

Dream Design

The Dream Design Mandala template is a tool for dimensionalizing intended outcomes: magnetizing specific realities into being. In the template, you will make a small, neutral, mono-color energy sketch of the current starting point. Then, with arrows pointing toward the main event (your dimensionalization), you will draw your dream design in full color and detail as a manifested "future", now a reality. The focus is the fruition of a best possible outcome, mapped in the same circle of potentiality.

The Dream Design should pop off the page with its color and energy. Remember the power of this tool is "seeing it" drawn as a reality, "believing it" as a potential that can come into form; and then "acting on it". You can draw inspiration from your Inquiries, Source Creations and Empowered Action prompts. Remember to energize the journal content with loving attention in meditation and with action in daily life.   It is an art to cocreate with the Quantum yet surrender outcomes. Trust that the power of life will organize what is in your highest and best good, whether it matches your pictures or not. Trust in a Divine, higher order and enjoy the experimentation.

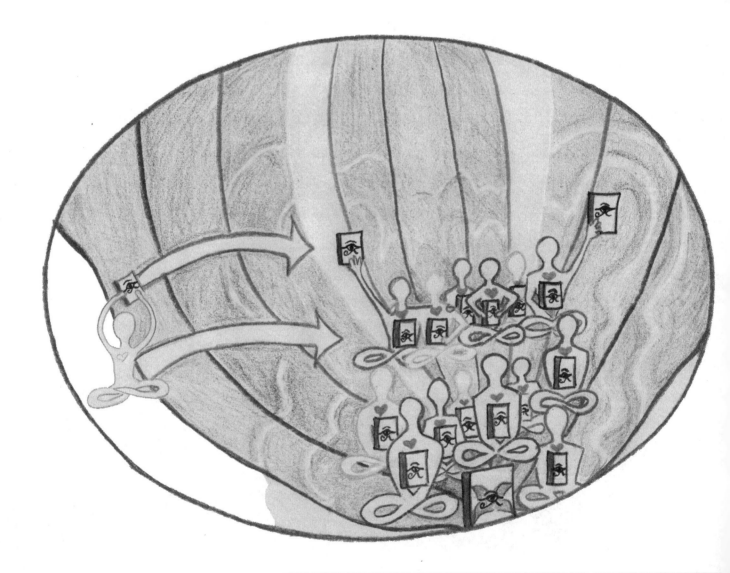

Everyday Magnificent: Life Practices

These tools are geared towards cultivating a living meditation practice that activates our unlimited nature.

Meditation is a gift we give ourselves and a way we can contribute to the collective field. One definition of meditation, that I love, is "to become familiar with". When we unplug from excessive external stimuli and hypnotic driving forces in our environment, we can become familiar with the Mystery of our own being. Some call it our quiet, still center, others refer to it as Buddha nature, the voice of God within, union, emptiness, mindfulness, the vast field of potential, etc.

By all names and methods, the practice of familiarizing ourselves with the state of stillness, silence, and wholeness, is a gateway to our unlimited nature. There are several meditation options detailed in this section, most of which evolve from four basic postures. Elaborate with your own variations. Remember it is not the amount of time in meditation that matters, as much as the quality of attention, consistency of practice, and the states we are able to access and sustain as we make contact with the Field.

Seated Meditation
Sit upright, with eyes closed, and bring attention and awareness to the present moment. Some seated meditation practices follow breath, others mantra (repetition of ancient prayers or invocations), while others focus on observation of space, body sensation or developing witness state. Use your favorite method/s and integrate new ones to expand your practice.

Standing Meditation
Standing meditation helps to cultivate balance, presence, strength and focus. With eyes open, (or closed), use it to expand 360 degree awareness. Feel the strength of your body, vertically connecting to the life force of the Earth beneath you and the Cosmos above you. Imagine your spine as a conduit, like connective tissue between the "Heavens and Earth".

Moving Meditation
In movement, we generate, integrate and circulate energy. Bringing attention and presence to our movement, amplifies energy and increases embodied awareness. Moving meditations may include walking, athletics, dance, martial arts, and energy medicine practices, such as Yoga or Chi Gong.

Reclining Meditation
In this position of receptivity, our autonomic nervous system can naturally restore and recalibrate. The reclining meditation is a wonderful way to integrate and settle. Savasana, the "corpse" pose from the yoga tradition, exemplifies the value of this meditation. The key here is surrender, letting go and being held in the Unified Field.

The following practices integrate variations of the four meditation postures along with other expressive arts meditation practices. They are offered as starting points. Use them to inspire your exploration, and experiment with creating your own variations. Practice daily to expand your awareness and accelerate your Everyday Magnificent journey. Over time, intentional awareness can give most every form of daily sitting, standing, moving and reclining a quality of living meditation. Start where you are, as you are; with loving compassion. *We suggest beginning all meditation practices with some version of Intentional Breathing and Unity Coherence.*

Intentional Breathing

Begin all activities, practices and touchstones in this journal by focusing on the breath. Begin with taking 10 relaxed, deep breaths. Build up to a practice of 5-10 minutes of full, steady breathing. Try increasing the length of inhale and exhales over a count of 5 seconds. Allow a circular breath pattern to emerge. If attention wanders with thought forms or feelings, return to the sensation of the breath, breathing you.

When fatigued, anxious or frustrated, pause and take 5 of these steady, full breaths and notice if your energy shifts to a more relaxed and spacious state. Experiment with breathing techniques from favorite yoga or healing arts practices. Deepen your intimate relationship and commitment to intentional breathing. Allow breath to circulate and replenish your being. Many wisdom traditions say, "breath is life". It is a direct path to revitalizing and optimizing the health of body, mind, spirit.

Unity Coherence

In a seated posture, close your eyes, center with your breath and relax your body. Breathe with steady, full inhalations and exhalations. Allow your breath to become rhythmic and circular. Bring attention to your chest, as if the breath is moving in and out through the center of your chest. Keep attention on your heart center as you breathe. Begin to elevate your state by generating the emotion of gratitude. Bring to awareness anything for which you feel grateful.

Expand this awareness from your heart in every direction. Imagine gratitude radiating with each generous breath. Now circulate this state by breathing it through your whole body and energetic field. Extend a state of relaxed wholeness and communion with all life. Feel held, breathed and carried in the web of life; the Unified Field.

See and feel your whole being fueled and circulating loving, coherent energy: steep, absorb, regenerate. Flood your whole brain and nervous system with this unified, coherent energy. Radiate this coherent energy to all beings and all life. Continue this practice for 5 to 10 minutes. Revisit it often. At first it may take repeated practice to establish and maintain a state of coherence. With consistent practice, Unity Coherence can be activated and sustained throughout the day.

Making Intentional Breathing and Unity Coherence baseline practices (repeated often) will better serve your Everyday Magnificent journey (visit www.heartmath.com for heart coherence info).

Walking Meditation

Take a walk outside, connecting to the ground beneath you and the sky above. If possible, walk barefoot on the ground to better entrain to the frequency of the Earth. Feel your body as an extension of the Earth and Cosmos. Breathe and connect with the life force animating all life. Imagine your whole nervous system opening and drinking in the intelligence of the Unified Field. Offer gratitude. Observe life around you and feel yourself intimately connected to all things and all beings. As you continue walking, reflect upon and energize the details of your Source Creations and Dream Designs. Generate an elevated emotional state of love and gratitude for the potentials you are magnetizing that already exist in the Quantum Field. Embody these potentials and walk into their reality. Broadcast an electromagnetic signature of unity, coherence and gratitude. When you feel complete, give thanks and surrender all outcomes into the Unknown.

Dancing Meditation

Center in stillness. Begin to move (to music or in silence). Move authentically. Breathe and connect with the energy animating all life. Feel yourself connected to all things and all beings. Allow the energy of spontaneity and playfulness to move you. Let the dance inhabit you. Reflect upon and energize the content of your Source Creations and Dream Designs. Visualize the life you are designing as a present moment reality. Generate an elevated emotional state of love and gratitude for how it feels to live your "dream" reality and dance these potentials into being. As you complete, surrender your experience to the intelligence of the Unified Field. If you are able, lie down and take a few minutes to integrate in a reclining meditation.

Vocalize: Tone-Chant-Sing

As you get comfortable with breathing practices, experiment with vocalizing, toning and resonating sounds on the exhale. Improvise or practice one of many forms of toning and chanting. You may try integrating Sanskrit mantras (which resonate electromagnetic signatures of unity, wholeness and love). You may prefer to sing songs you love, or make up your own. Allow your voice to sound and reverberate. Allow energy to move! Don't stop if you hit resistance. Instead, keep going beyond the edge of your comfort zone. Remember, we are exploring the unknown and unconventional. Tears may come or bursts of cathartic energy. Allow the process. Give sound to your soul, to your prayers. Play with vocal range and ride waves of sound and vibration. Experiment till tones drop into silence. Offer gratitude and linger in the silence as long as you are able.

Soul Dance: Vibrate-Shake-Elevate

Play music that inspires your body to move. Walk, dance and wiggle, letting your limbs and spine move fluidly. Allow spontaneous, free movement to dislodge stuck energy. Release tension and let your dance bring you to life. Tremble, vibrate, shake, flow, groove. Follow the joy of movement as you embody melody and rhythm. Use the dance to liberate, elevate and energize your emotional state. Visualize and embody your best self and best life as you move. Ride the dance into the Unknown and surrender into the moment. Be free. At the height of the experience, offer gratitude for your life and naturally wind down. Lie down, sit or stand in stillness, sensing your heartbeat and breath. If any guidance or insights come to you, grab for your journal as you complete and write them down.

Nature Sit

Practice seated meditation with eyes open or closed in an outdoor nature space. This location can change with every sitting, or you may revisit a favorite location. Entrain to the frequencies of the natural world and immerse in the energy of the elements all around you. Be receptive as the creatures and plants in this space nourish you and model *being*. Receive them as wise teachers. Attune to the earth, sun wind, water and natural cycles. Surrender; harmonize your nervous system to the orchestration of the natural world. Offer gratitude and radiate your elevated state to nourish all life. Rest in the Unified Field, and let it hold you. Sit with focused presence and attention for at least 10-20 minutes. Drink it in.

Make Music

Music is vibration; an immediate immersion into the waves of the Quantum Field. Pick up and play an instrument of any kind, from percussion, keyboard, flute, guitar or even your own voice. If all you have are your hands clapping, or fingers snapping, that's OK. Surrender to the music within and let it move you and move through you. Immerse in the experience. Notice resistance or belief that you are not musical and choose beyond voices of the inner critic. Be playful. Become frequency, wave, rhythm and melody. Lose yourself in music. Let it surprise you.

Energy Medicine Bundle

There are infinite practices for activating and optimizing the energetic body. Here are a few to get started. Play with them, research new ones and add your own. These practices are doorways into the central nervous system, the operating system that wires and nourishes the whole of our being. These can be practiced sequentially or as single touchstones anywhere, anytime.

Many ancient traditions including Yoga and Asian Medicine are rich with practices and material for study and application. Expand your repertoire; find what you love and get flowing!

Thymus Thump

Center awareness with your breath and using finger tips, begin gently thumping your thymus (heart, chest area). You can use both hands or just one. Thump all along your collarbone. Inhale and exhale deeply through the mouth. Relax your jaw. Gently open your mouth and allow an "Aaaaaaah…" sound to resonate as you thump and breathe. Repeat for 30 seconds or more.

Tapping

Tap the center point of your outer palms together (where you would make a "karate chop") and breathe deeply, repeating silently or out loud, "I am willing to be clear." This is similar to the "thump", but a bit more gentle. Using index and middle fingers, tap the crown of the head on both right and left sides. Tap temples, third eye area, bony protrusion under the eyes, and outer cheekbones. Continue to tap the jaw, above lips and on the chin. Breathe deeply as you tap, surrender and let go. This simple practice opens pathways to circulate energy and clear blockages in the system. No need to over think or understand, just breathe, tap and trust. Then move on with your day!

Kneading and Squeezing

Use one hand and then the other to massage your own hands, fingers, forearms and upper arms. With extra time, you might extend this practice to include your ears, feet, calves and shins. Use your thumb and finger tips to massage pressure points along meridians where energy flows. Gently dig in as if kneading dough. Lovingly release tension with breath; exhaling as you knead and squeeze tissue along the bones. You will naturally stimulate circulation of blood and activate energy pathways. Hold the intention that depleted areas of your body receive a flood of life force, and see over active or stuck areas becoming regulated and harmonized. Become aware of subtle energies and trust your intuitive sense to guide this self-healing practice.

Open Circuit

Place an index finger on the third eye center (middle of the forehead) and an index finger in your navel. Gently press in and upwards for a count of 15 seconds. Inhale through the nose and allow a gentle sighing breath (with an audible sigh) through an open mouth. Visualize a circuit activating, connecting all your centers with flowing energy. Open to the flow of the Unified Field and receive the communion of, "My Will and Thy Will, as One." Invite and direct energy to circulate life force. Breathe wholeness, connection. Repeat this 3 times. Offer gratitude and move on.

Quantum Wildcard Practices

Reality Artist Vows

Write Reality Artist vows. Compose these vows from your heart and let them reveal your soul's voice and your commitment to life. Use this exercise as a way to devote yourself to and honor a life of love and authentic presence. It is a declaration, and standard for your accountability. Once complete, type, print, and post it where you will read it daily. Live into it, and live up to it.

Example:

As a Reality Artist,
I vow to keep my attention on the Unified Field
To sing, dance and live from the inside out
Weaving devotional art of this whole precious life
I vow to surrender, flooding grace and laughter
Into a river of freedom and an ocean of bliss
In which all beings may be replenished
I vow to inspire, uplift and serve all life
To be utilized as a force of unconditional, evolutionary love
Birthing creations of wholeness
I vow to be unlimited, free
Devoted to a miraculous, magnificent life of Love.

Love Letter

Write a letter to your current self from your future/eternal self. Choose a specific topic or inquiry you feel curiosity about or an area which is challenging you (where the trusted counsel of an elder or mentor is welcome). Write as the future/eternal self, to your current self and allow loving wisdom to emerge. Go beyond default responses in your writing. Allow your letter to flow from the Quantum, the Unknown. What would this wise one want you to know? What would it want you to remember about your unlimited nature? What does it have to tell you about living into an Everyday Magnificent reality? What wisdom is offered to live more wholly as your evolved future self? Be sure to offer loving gratitude to your current and future selves. Reread this letter. Mail it to yourself and receive it anew when it arrives. Most importantly, put this sage counsel to practice in your daily life.

Dream Assignment

Make this the last thing you do before drifting off to sleep. On a pad of paper or Open Reflection page of your journal (that you will leave at your bedside with a pen), write a version of the following note.

Dear Quantum Field (or address it as you prefer);
Thank you so much for the gift of life. I am so grateful! I love you and am available to receive the most direct and useful insight and experiences to better serve my living. If it is in the highest good, please send me a dream or mystical experience tonight, that gives me insight into the following inquiry, (Insert your inquiry or topic here.) Please help me to remember this experience clearly, and to record it as relevant, useful information upon awakening. Thank you so much. I surrender outcomes and offer my best to life.
Love, (your name)

As you complete, turn off the light, and drift off to sleep. The moment you awaken, write down anything that you remember from your sleeping/dreaming state. Repeat this assignment nightly until you feel you have received a relevant response to your inquiry. Then, put the wisdom from your response into action in your life.

Life Art

Make cooking and nourishing yourself and others a meditation practice. Prepare food in a loving, mindful meditative state. Use the selection of ingredients, preparation and presentation as a ritual of nourishment. Pay attention to your breath, thoughts and emotions through the process of food preparation. Give thanks for the ingredients and generate elevated states of love, joy and gratitude as you prepare the meal. Use color, design and beauty to embellish the presentation. From creation, to enjoyment of sharing, eating and digestion make the entire experience living art. Have fun with it. Light a candle, arrange flowers, and create a space to honor life. Where else in your life can you apply this life art practice? In your professional work? Parenting? In relationships with partners, lovers, elders? How can you show up to all your daily activities, even the seemingly mundane, with an awareness of creativity, beauty, nourishment and sacred attention? Be a life artist!

Earth Art

Begin with a Nature Sit meditation. Ask for a blessing to use found objects to create an intentional offering or prayer. Only after you sense a "yes", stand up and gather materials for your Earth Art. Allow the beauty of the natural space to inform you. Collect items without disrupting the natural balance of the space. Tread with sensitivity and awareness. Allow your creative inspiration to guide you as you create your offering. You can create with sticks, pine cones, stones, leaves and whatever you find. You can create a mandala, a circle of stones, a spiral of leaves, a nest - the possibilities are endless. Let the moment and the Mystery guide you. You may choose to be empty and present to the subtleties of the moment, and/or to create with an area of inquiry, challenge or prayer held in your awareness. Allow the process of communing with Earth , creativity and beauty to be healing, revolutionary. When you feel complete, give thanks; and surrender your offering back to the cycles of nature.

Touchstones

These tools can be accessed on the spot; anywhere, anytime.

Touchstones are designed to take 1 to 5 minutes and serve as state shifts and reminders to activate your unlimited nature. With repeated practice, they become second nature and enrich Everyday Magnificent living. Practice your touchstone 1-3x a day.

Circulate-Radiate

Practice Intentional Breath and Unity Coherence. In this activated state, circulate and radiate the emotions of unconditional love, gratitude and joy. Allow these energies to bubble up authentically within you. Circulate and radiate this elevated energy within you and all around you. Broadcast and direct it to loved ones or the Earth itself. Smile. Breathe. Offer gratitude.

Broadcast Infinity

Presence yourself in breath and heart. Activate Unity Coherence. Circulate this state of wholeness through your entire body. Imagine a luminous stream of energy in the form of an infinity symbol, emanating like ripples throughout your blood stream. See it flowing through your spinal fluid. See it bathing every cell of your organs, muscle, tissue and bones. Broadcast this infinity symbol in every direction, through your nervous system and then into the space beyond your body. Breathe infinity, walk infinity. Make the gesture of the sacred symbol with your hands over your energy centers. Give the loving invitation to each of your energy centers to activate, circulate and optimize with infinite unconditional love and wisdom. Bless all that is around you with the sacred symbol and broadcast infinity with 360 degree awareness.

Pause and Surrender

Build on the practice of Intentional Breathing. Relaxing into a steady flow of breath, close your eyes and notice the darkness. Unplug from external sight and look within. Invite the quality of life that is Mystery and lean into the Unknown, tuning into subtle vibrations. Notice distractions or resistance and move beyond them. Become friends with the dark, feeling safe, whole and free there. Utilize these simple pauses to surrender all you think you know. Pause thinking and deepen intimate relationship to the unseen energies of life. Surrender into the Unknown and fall in love with this vast space. Several times a day, pause and ask "Am I surrendered to the current of the Unknown? Or am I driving through my mind's agenda?" As needed, adjust. Pause, Surrender. Flow.

Flood the YES

As soon as you sense yourself waking in the morning, before "thinking" sets in, flood your energy field with the awareness of your unlimited nature. Flood your field with the feeling of being in love with your life. Activate Unity Coherence and circulate/radiate a "YES" to life. How does this YES feel? How does it respond to the day before you? What choices will it make? How will it meet whatever arises? Generate the elevated emotion of this YES, and flood it through your entire system. Broadcast it into your day. Keep it playful, childlike. Throughout your day, remember to flood your awareness with your YES. Return to it every time you notice distraction, or indulgence in negativity or stress. Smile and breathe your YES into life.

Flood Gratitude

As you close your eyes to drift off to sleep, give thanks! Relax in reclining meditation, finding comfort in your body and deepening your breath. Activate Unity Coherence. Flood your awareness with gratitude and direct this energy to circulate throughout your entire nervous system. Invite all your energy centers to wash with the elevated emotion of gratitude. See and feel gratitude flooding your organs and regenerating your tissue, muscle, bones. If you have any injuries or areas of illness, flood them with a wash of wholesome, grateful love. Put your whole self to rest in the intelligent love of the Quantum Field. Review your Source Creations and Dream Designs, and see them manifest. Generate and flood gratitude for your answered prayers . Gently, gratefully surrender into the loving arms of the Universe and drift off to sleep.

Drink in the Quantum

Fill a tall glass of fresh water. As you lift it up to your lips, envision it filled with the vibrations of unconditional love and wholeness. Consciously drink in this pure nourishment from the deepest well of Creation. Use this touchstone as a ritual to expand the place from which you are breathing, being, and literally drinking in life force energy. Drink in connection and communion with the creative, animating force of life. Drink in direct guidance, safety and trust. Drink in nourishment, remembrance, freedom. Let it quench your thirst for the sacred. Abide in this unconditional love from the inside out as every cell drinks in the Quantum.

Juicy Spine

Standing, seated or on all fours gently begin to undulate the spine. Move slowly and pay attention to every vertebrae - from the tail all the way to the cervical and crown of the head. Visualize and move with the fluidity of the tail of a kite in the sky or a snake in motion. Breathe deeply. Improvise your movement allowing mindful, embodied awareness to guide you. Flood your spine with breath and gentle, nurturing movement. Offer gratitude for your supple, vital spine.

Jump for Joy

Set a timer, (start with one minute and build up to 5). Begin to jump for joy! Hoot, holler, laugh, happy dance. Skip, run and jump, making vocal and facial expressions of ecstatic joy and happiness. Be silly, goofy, and free. Notice resistances and keep going. Bust out of programmed and conditioned ideas of what is normal or acceptable. Speak out loud and vocalize prayers, intentions, gratitudes. Bless everything. Does this elevate your state? How does this few minutes of uncensored joy and freedom inform the rest of your day? How does it impact your well being and aliveness?

Catch and Shift

This practice invites unconscious patterns to become conscious so you can *Catch and Shift* them. Become aware of habitual thinking or feeling. This might include analytical thinking (polarized good/bad, right/wrong), or indulging in emotional conditioning that produces a familiar loop, old story or downward spiral. As you bring awareness of these tendencies to the surface, you have the power to redirect energy in the present moment and rewire, creating new experiences.

The moment you catch feelings or thought forms that are diminishing your life force, stop. Pause, shift and reset. Begin by stepping back into the present moment: find something to appreciate or feel grateful for in your life, right now. Smile, breathe deeply. Activate Unity Coherence. Be grateful for your increasing awareness and celebrate your willingness to change conditioned programs and shift your energy into evolutionary love and freedom.

Authentic Movement

Begin in stillness with eyes closed. Sense and follow your movement impulses. Allow breath to inspire gesture. Begin to move with your gesture and let it extend into larger movement. Be spontaneous. You are tapping into innate body wisdom beyond "thinking" mind. Let it guide you. Authentic movement naturally reveals treasures of self healing. This practice often releases stuck energy. It soothes, restores and energizes us in ways that externally imposed movement may not provide.

Joint Spiral

Begin by circulating breath through your body, then systemically begin to circle and spiral every joint. Move from the base of the feet to the top of the head. Include your toes and fingers, ankles, wrists, knees, elbows, hips, shoulders, and spine. Lengthen arms to the sky and make big circles. Feed your joints with breath and feel synovial fluid replenishing your joints with every spiral movement. While moving, generate the elevated state of gratitude. Visualize liquid love flowing through your whole body, and give thanks for your vitality, supple body and strength.

Sacred Interruptions

Set 3 to 5 alarms on your phone daily as reminders to practice Touchstones. Use favorite songs (as alarm ring tones) that inspire you to generate elevated states of unlimited gratitude, love, happiness, abundance, etc. Give your alarms clear, concise names that will flash across your phone or device. Every time an alarm goes off, take 1-3 minutes and practice the activity or focus for which your alarm was set. Allow these moments to nourish you. They interrupt the hypnotic trance of old patterns and connect you back to your unlimited nature.

Sacred interruptions serve as a reset and uplift to your day. They should only require a few minutes, and allow you to return to your work-life flow refreshed and focused. Explore a few every week. Sacred Interruptions can also be organic, 'without device' reminders. For example, pause and practice touchstones at sunrise, mid day and sunset. Create your own sacred interruptions! Experiment and have fun.

Example:

9:00am	*Drink in the Quantum*
Noon	*Dance Song-Energize*
4:30pm	*Thymus Tap*
10:00pm	*Flood Gratitude*

Everyday Magnificent Journal

Practice: Intentional Breathing | Pg. 16
Touchstone: Broadcast Infinity | Pg. 22

ACTIVITY: Gratitude and Synchronicity | Pg. 10

ACTIVITY: To Be List | Pg. 11

Practice: Unity Coherence | Pg. 16
Touchstone: Circulate-Radiate | Pg. 22

ACTIVITY: Free Write, Inquiry Prompt | Pg. 10

What is my current vision for my most inspired life? (If you don't have one, create it!) In this vision, how do I live, what do I do? How do I feel? What and whom surrounds me? What is my "YES" to life? How does (or would) this "YES" inspire and motivate my daily living?

Everyday Magnificent | Date: _____

Practice: Walking Meditation | Pg. 17
Touchstone: Flood the Yes! | Pg. 22
ACTIVITY: Single Mandala | Pg. 12

Open Reflection | Pg. 11

Everyday Magnificent | Date: _____

Practice: Seated Meditation | Pg. 15
Touchstone: Flood Gratitude | Pg. 23

ACTIVITY: Free Write, Inquiry Prompt | Pg. 10
What is my innate genius, unique essential spark? How do I share it already? How else do I long to express it through my living and loving?

Practice: Intentional Breathing | Pg. 16
Touchstone: Jump For Joy | Pg. 24

ACTIVITY: Source Creations | Pg. 11

Empowered Actions | Pg. 11

Everyday Magnificent | Date: _____

Practice: Energy Medicine Bundle | Pg. 18, 19
Touchstone: Pause and Surrender | Pg. 22

ACTIVITY: Free Write, Inquiry Prompt | Pg. 10
When do I feel the most inspired, unlimited and unstoppable? (write about moments in the past, present or future. Include full sensory details: feelings, sights, sounds. Include states of being, actions and experiences).

Open Reflection | Pg. 11

Everyday Magnificent | Date: _____

Practice: Standing or Seated Meditation | Pg. 15
Touchstone: Juicy Spine | Pg. 23

ACTIVITY: Mandala Series | Pg. 12

Everyday Magnificent | Date: _____

Practice: Dancing Meditation | Pg. 17
Touchstone: Drink in the Quantum | Pg. 23

ACTIVITY: Free Write, Inquiry Prompt | Pg. 10
What do I feel passionate about these days? What most lights me up and how does it inform my life calling at this stage of my life?

Everyday Magnificent | Date: _____

Practice: Nature Sit | Pg. 18
Touchstone: Pause-Surrender | Pg. 22
ACTIVITY: Dream Design | Pg. 14

Open Reflection | Pg. 11

Everyday Magnificent | Date: _____

Practice: Energy Medicine Bundle | Pg. 18, 19
Touchstone: Broadcast Infinity | Pg. 22

ACTIVITY: Quantum Wild Card -Reality Artist Vows | Pg. 20

Open Reflection | Pg. 11

Everyday Magnificent | Date: _____

Practice: Make Music | Pg. 23
Touchstone: Flood Gratitude | Pg. 18

ACTIVITY: Mandala Series | Pg. 12

Everyday Magnificent | Date: _____

Practice: Reclining Meditation | Pg. 15
Touchstone: Flood the Yes | Pg. 22

ACTIVITY: Distillation | Pg. 11

Everyday Magnificent | Date: _____

Practice: Walking Meditation | Pg. 17
Touchstone: Catch and Shift | Pg. 24

ACTIVITY: Single Mandala | Pg. 12

Practice: Vocalize: Tone-Chant-Sing | Pg. 17
Touchstone: Sacred Interruptions | Pg. 25

ACTIVITY: Gratitude and Synchronicity | Pg. 11

ACTIVITY: To Be List | Pg. 11

Everyday Magnificent | Date: _____

Practice: Soul Dance | Pg. 17
Touchstone: Authentic Movement | Pg. 24

ACTIVITY: Free Write, Inquiry Prompt | Pg. 10
Where and how do I notice the flow of Energy and awareness increasing in my life?
How is my relationship to my unlimited nature expanding?

Open Reflection | Pg. 11

Everyday Magnificent | Date: _____

Practice: Make Music | Pg. 18
Touchstone: Pause-Surrender | Pg. 22

ACTIVITY: Gratitude and Synchronicity | Pg. 10

ACTIVITY: To Be List | Pg. 11

Everyday Magnificent | Date: _____

Open Reflection | Pg. 11

Everyday Magnificent | Date: _____

Practice: Seated Meditation | Pg. 15
Touchstone: Joint Spiral | Pg. 25

ACTIVITY: Dream Design | Pg. 114

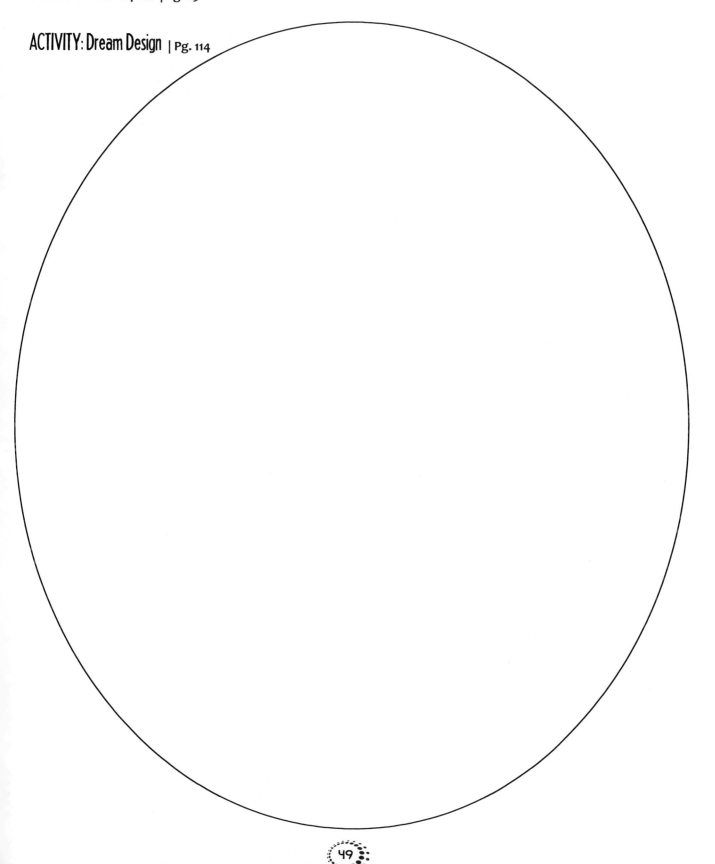

Everyday Magnificent | Date: _____

Open Reflection | Pg. 11

Everyday Magnificent | Date: _____

Practice: Dancing Meditation | Pg. 17
Touchstone: Circulate-Radiate | Pg. 22

ACTIVITY: Source Creations | Pg. 11

ACTIVITY: Empowered Actions | Pg. 11

•

Open Reflection | Pg. 11

Everyday Magnificent | Date: _____

Practice: Quantum Wild Card - Life Art | Pg. 21
Touchstone: Catch and Shift | Pg. 24

ACTIVITY: Single Mandala | Pg. 12

Open Reflection | Pg. 11

Everyday Magnificent | Date: _____

Practice: Walking Meditation | Pg. 17
Touchstone: Flood the YES | Pg. 22

ACTIVITY: Distillation | Pg. 14

Open Reflection | Pg. 11

Everyday Magnificent | Date: _____

Practice: Nature Sit | Pg. 18
Touchstone: Juicy Spine | Pg. 23

ACTIVITY: Free Write, Inquiry Prompt | Pg. 10

Describe your routines, habitual, movements, language, behaviors, thoughts, feelings, moods, etc. Which of these serve growth and which have become limiting or automatic in degenerative ways? Playfully redesign. What are some new ways of moving, speaking, feeling, being and relating? Write them here and put it to practice.

Open Reflection | Pg. 11

Everyday Magnificent | Date: _____

Practice: Unity Coherence | Pg. 16
Touchstone: Joint Spiral | Pg. 25

ACTIVITY: Free Write, Inquiry Prompt | Pg. 10

When I feel at my best; present and happy from the inside out, how do I move through my days, the world? How do I or would I sense and experience the world living from this place?

Open Reflection | Pg. 11

Everyday Magnificent | Date: _____

Practice: Seated or Reclining Meditation | Pg. 15
Touchstone: Flood the Yes | Pg. 22

ACTIVITY: Mandala Series | Pg. 12

Open Reflection | Pg. 11

Everyday Magnificent | Date: _____

Practice: Intentional Breathing, Unity Coherence | Pg. 16
Touchstone: Sacred Interruptions | Pg. 25

ACTIVITY: Free Write, Inquiry Prompt | Pg. 10
How does living, feeling and being magnificent feel to me? What does my life look and feel like when I am living my magnificence? How can I more fully live this into daily life?

Everyday Magnificent | Date: _____

Open Reflection | Pg. 11

Everyday Magnificent I Date: _____

Practice: Vocalize, Tone, Chant, Sing | Pg. 17
Touchstone: Jump for Joy | Pg. 24

ACTIVITY: Mandala Series | Pg. 12

Open Reflection | Pg. 11

Everyday Magnificent I Date: _____

Practice: Soul Dance, Quantum Wild Card - Dream Assignment | Pg. 17, 24
Touchstone: Broadcast Infinity | Pg. 22

ACTIVITY: Distillation | Pg. 11

Open Reflection | Pg. 11

Everyday Magnificent | Date: _____

Practice: Seated or Reclining Meditation | Pg. 15
Touchstone: Juicy Spine | Pg. 23

ACTIVITY: Gratitude and Synchronicity | Pg. 10

ACTIVITY: To Be List | Pg. 11

Everyday Magnificent | Date: _____

Open Reflection | Pg. 11

Everyday Magnificent | Date: _____

Practice: Make Music | Pg. 18
Touchstone: Flood Gratitude | Pg. 23

ACTIVITY: Single Mandala | Pg. 12

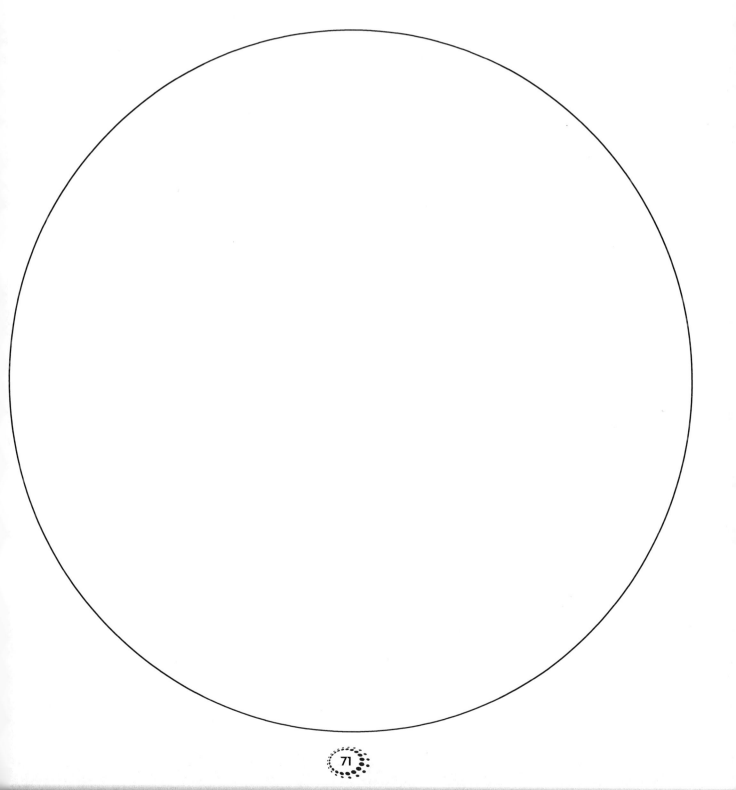

Open Reflection | Pg. 11

Everyday Magnificent I Date: _____

Practice: Seated Meditation | Pg. 15
Touchstone: Catch and Shift | Pg. 24

ACTIVITY: Free Write , Inquiry Prompt | Pg. 10
What am I learning about my unlimited nature and how to let it guide my life?

Open Reflection | Pg. 11

Practice: Four Fold Meditation of Your Choice (integrate 5 minutes of each) | Pg. 15
Touchstone: Authentic Movement | Pg. 23

ACTIVITY: Source Goals | Pg. 11

ACTIVITY: Empowered Actions | Pg. 11

Open Reflection | Pg. 11

Everyday Magnificent | Date: _____

Practice: Unity Coherence with Reclining Meditation | Pg. 15, 16
Touchstone: Sacred Interruptions | Pg. 25

ACTIVITY: Dream Design | Pg. 12

Everyday Magnificent I Date: _____

Open Reflection | Pg. 11

Everyday Magnificent | Date: _____

Practice: Nature Sit, Earth Art | Pg. 18, 21
Touchstone: Juicy Spine | Pg. 23

ACTIVITY: Free Write, Inquiry Prompt | Pg. 10
In what new ways do I feel inspired to develop, build or create that are also a contribution to the whole of local and planetary community well being?

Open Reflection | Pg. 11

Everyday Magnificent | Date: _____

Practice: Four Fold Meditation (Integrate 5 minutes of each) | Pg. 15
Touchstone: Drink in the Quantum | Pg. 23

ACTIVITY: Mandala Series | Pg. 12

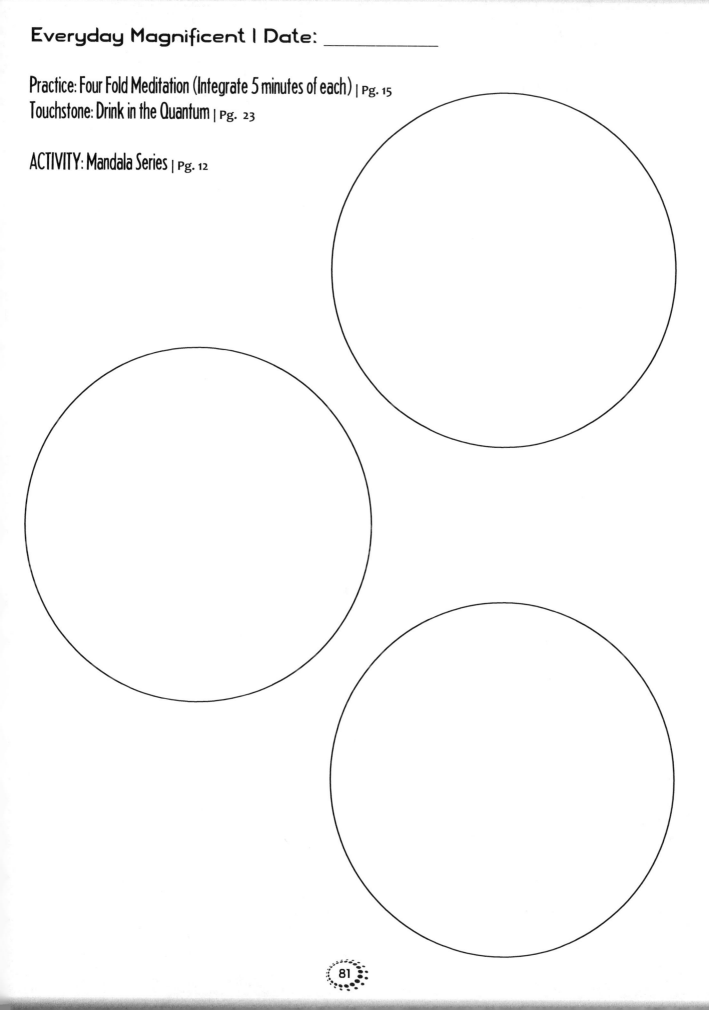

Open Reflection | Pg. 11

Everyday Magnificent | Date: _____

Practice: Energy Medicine Bundle in Standing Meditation | Pg. 18, 19, 15
Touchstone: Authentic Movement | Pg. 24

ACTIVITY: Distillation | Pg. 11

Everyday Magnificent | Date: _____

Open Reflection | Pg. 11

Everyday Magnificent | Date: _____

Practice: Movement Meditation, Quantum Wild Card - Life Art | Pg. 15, 21
Touchstone: Flood the Yes | Pg. 22

ACTIVITY: Gratitude and Synchronicity | Pg. 10

ACTIVITY: To Be List | Pg. 11

Open Reflection | Pg. 11

Everyday Magnificent | Date: _____

Practice: Seated Meditation | Pg. 15
Touchstone: Drink In The Quantum | Pg. 23

ACTIVITY: Single Mandala | Pg. 12

Everyday Magnificent | Date: _____

Open Reflection | Pg. 11

Everyday Magnificent | Date: _____

Practice: Nature Sit | Pg. 18
Touchstone: Jump for Joy | Pg. 24

ACTIVITY: Free Write, Inquiry Prompt | Pg. 10
What do I appreciate about my essential being?

Everyday Magnificent | Date: _____

Practice: Intentional Breathing with Seated Meditation | Pg. 17
Touchstone: Pause-Surrender | Pg. 22

ACTIVITY: Mandala Series | Pg. 12

Everyday Magnificent | Date: _____

Open Reflection | Pg. 11

Everyday Magnificent | Date: _____

Practice: Reclining Meditation | Pg. 15
Touchstone: Flood Gratitude | Pg. 23

ACTIVITY: Free Write, Inquiry Prompt | Pg. 10

What is the message from my eternal, wise self, at this point in my Everyday Magnificent journey? What does it most want me to remember and live into action?

Everyday Magnificent | Date: _____

Open Reflection | Pg. 11

Everyday Magnificent I Date: _____

Practice: Intentional Breathing, Unity Coherence in Seated Meditation | Pg. 15, 16
Touchstone: Pause-Surrender | Pg. 22

ACTIVITY: Mandala Series | Pg. 12

Open Reflection | Pg. 11

Everyday Magnificent I Date: _____

Practice: Nature Sit | Pg. 21
Touchstone: Joint Spiral and Juicy Spine | Pg. 22

ACTIVITY: Dream Design | Pg. 14

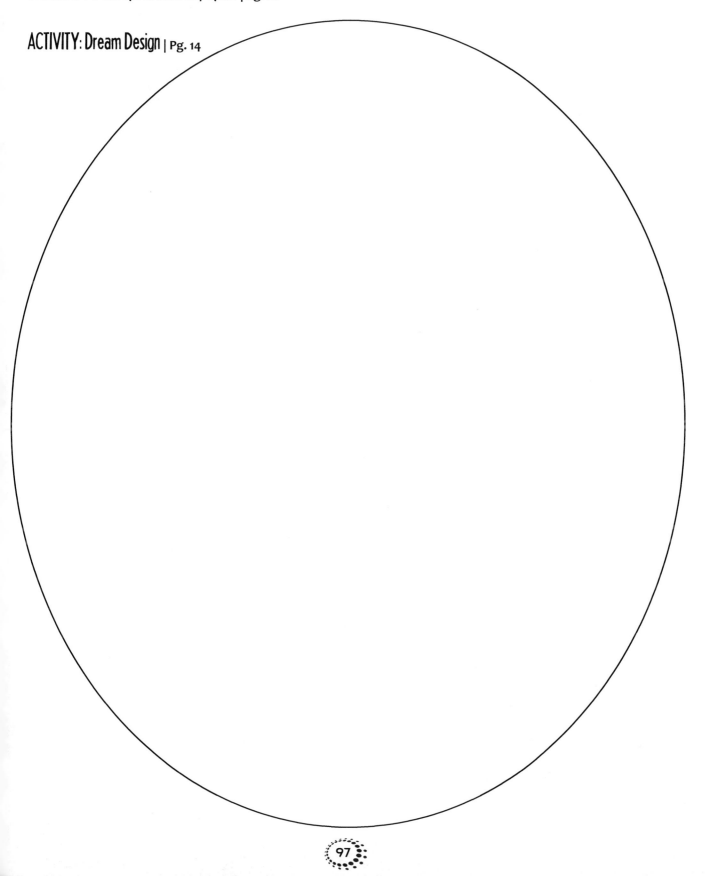

Open Reflection | Pg. 11

Practice: Earth Art | Pg. 21
Touchstone: Sacred Interruptions | Pg. 25

ACTIVITY: Quantum Wild Card: Love Letter | Pg. 20

Open Reflection | Pg. 11

Everyday Magnificent | Date: _____

Practice: Energy Medicine Bundle with Unity Coherence | Pg. 18, 19, 16
Touchstone: Authentic Movement | Pg. 24

ACTIVITY: Distillation | Pg. 11

Open Reflection | Pg. 11

Everyday Magnificent | Date: _____

Practice: Four Fold Meditation (Integrate 5 minutes of each), Dream Assignment | Pg. 15, 21
Touchstone: Flood Gratitude | Pg. 23

ACTIVITY: Mandala Series | Pg. 12

Open Reflection | Pg. 11

Everyday Magnificent | Date: _____

Practice: Dancing, then Reclining Meditation | Pg. 15, 17
Touchstone: Circulate-Radiate and Flood The Yes | Pg. 22, 23

ACTIVITY: Free Write, Inquiry Prompt | Pg. 10
What is the leading learning edge of my creative expression and relationship to the Unknown? In what areas of my life can I experience more creativity and surrender into the Unknown more fully?

Everyday Magnificent | Date: _____

Open Reflection | Pg. 11

Everyday Magnificent | Date: _____

Practice: Soul Dance | Pg. 17
Touchstone: Drink in the Quantum , Jump for Joy | Pg. 23, 24

ACTIVITY: Single Mandala | Pg. 12

Open Reflection | Pg. 11

Everyday Magnificent | Date: _____

Practice: Seated or Walking Meditation | Pg. 15, 17
Touchstone: Broadcast Infinity | Pg. 22

ACTIVITY: Free Write, Inquiry Prompt | Pg. 10
How am I nurtured by Silence; Music; Movement; Breath; and Nature? How do they reveal and express my unlimited nature?

Open Reflection | Pg. 11

Everyday Magnificent | Date: _____

Practice: Vocalize: Tone-Chant-Sing | Pg. 17
Touchstone: Joint Spiral | Pg. 25

ACTIVITY: Source Creations | Pg. 11

ACTIVITY: Empowered Actions | Pg. 11

Everyday Magnificent | Date: _____

Open Reflection | Pg. 11

Everyday Magnificent | Date: _____

Practice: Nature Sit and Earth Art | Pg. 18, 21
Touchstone: Circulate-Radiate and Flood Gratitude | Pg. 22, 23

ACTIVITY: Quantum Wild Card: Love Letter | Pg. 20

Everyday Magnificent | Date: _____

Open Reflection | Pg. 11

Everyday Magnificent I Date: _____

Practice: Unity Coherence | Pg. 16
Touchstone: Authentic Movement | Pg. 24

ACTIVITY: Distillation | Pg. 11

Open Reflection | Pg. 11

Everyday Magnificent | Date: _____

Practice: Walking Meditation | Pg. 17
Touchstone: Sacred Interruptions | Pg. 25

ACTIVITY: Dream Design | Pg. 14

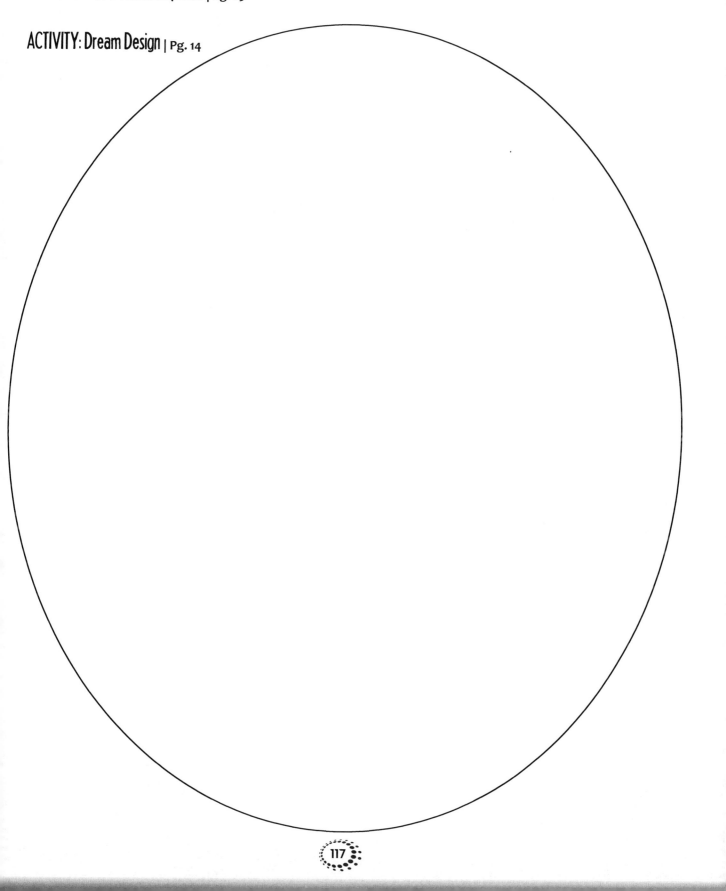

Open Reflection | Pg. 11

Everyday Magnificent | Date: _____

Practice: Seated Meditation | Pg. 15
Touchstone: Juicy Spine while Flooding Gratitude | Pg. 23

ACTIVITY: Gratitude and Synchronicity | Pg. 10

ACTIVITY: To Be List | Pg. 11

Open Reflection | Pg. 11

Everyday Magnificent | Date: _____

Practice: Soul Dance | Pg. 17
Touchstone: Flood the Yes | Pg. 22

ACTIVITY: Single Mandala | Pg. 12

Everyday Magnificent | Date: _____

Open Reflection | Pg. 11

Everyday Magnificent | Date: _____

Practice: Intentional Breath with Reclining Meditation | Pg. 15, 16
Touchstone: Pause and Surrender | Pg. 22

ACTIVITY: Free Write, Inquiry Prompt | Pg. 10
What current voice of my unlimited nature is emerging? What is its wisdom and how does it want me to live, love and contribute to life?

Open Reflection | Pg. 11

Everyday Magnificent | Date: _____

Practice: Walking Meditation with Unity Coherence | Pg. 15, 16
Touchstone: Catch and Shift | Pg. 24

ACTIVITY: Distillation | Pg. 11

Open Reflection | Pg. 11

Practice: Walking Meditation with Intentional Breathing | Pg. 16
Touchstone: Sacred Interruptions | Pg. 25

ACTIVITY: Source Creations | Pg. 11

ACTIVITY: Empowered Actions | Pg. 11

Everyday Magnificent | Date: _____

Open Reflection | Pg. 11

Everyday Magnificent | Date: _____

Practice: Energy Medicine Bundle, Life Art | Pg. 18, 19, 21
Touchstone: Flood Gratitude | Pg. 23

ACTIVITY: Mandala Series| Pg. 12

Open Reflection | Pg. 11

Practice: Make Music | Pg. 18
Touchstone: Authentic Movement | Pg. 24

ACTIVITY: Free Write, Inquiry Prompt | Pg. 10
What is sacred to me? How do I live a sacred life and what brings me into deeper communion with the creative source of life?

Open Reflection | Pg. 11

Everyday Magnificent | Date: _____

Practice: Dancing Meditation | Pg. 17
Touchstone: Juicy Spine | Pg. 23

ACTIVITY: Distillation | Pg. 11

Everyday Magnificent | Date: _____

Open Reflection | Pg. 11

Everyday Magnificent | Date: _____

Practice: Four Fold Meditation (integrate 5 minutes of each) | Pg. 15
Touchstone: Catch and Shift | Pg. 24

ACTIVITY: Single Mandala | Pg. 12

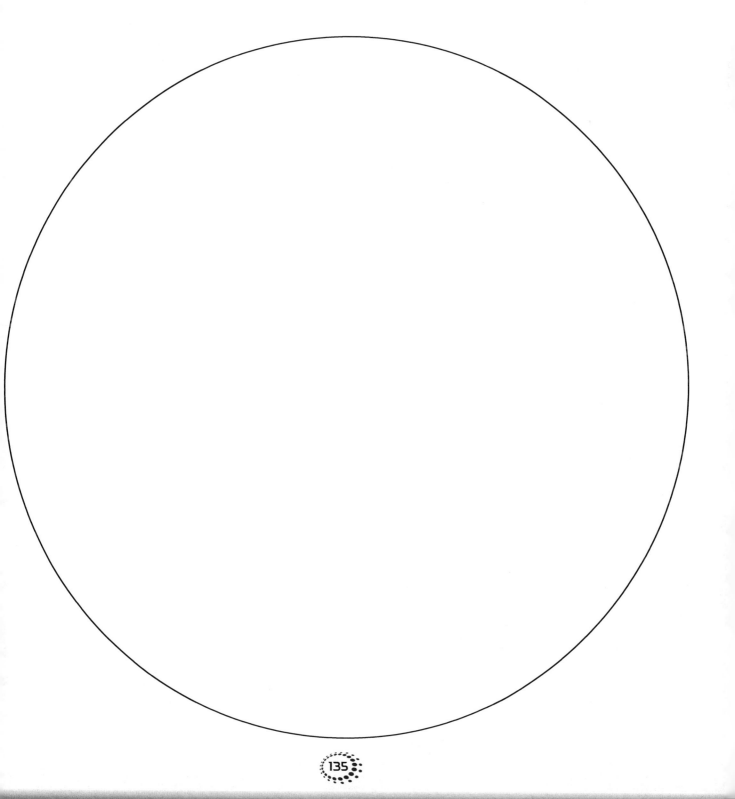

Open Reflection | Pg. 11

Everyday Magnificent | Date: _____

Practice: Soul Dance | Pg. 17
Touchstone: Joint Spiral and Juicy Spine | Pg. 24, 25

ACTIVITY: Dream Design | Pg. 14

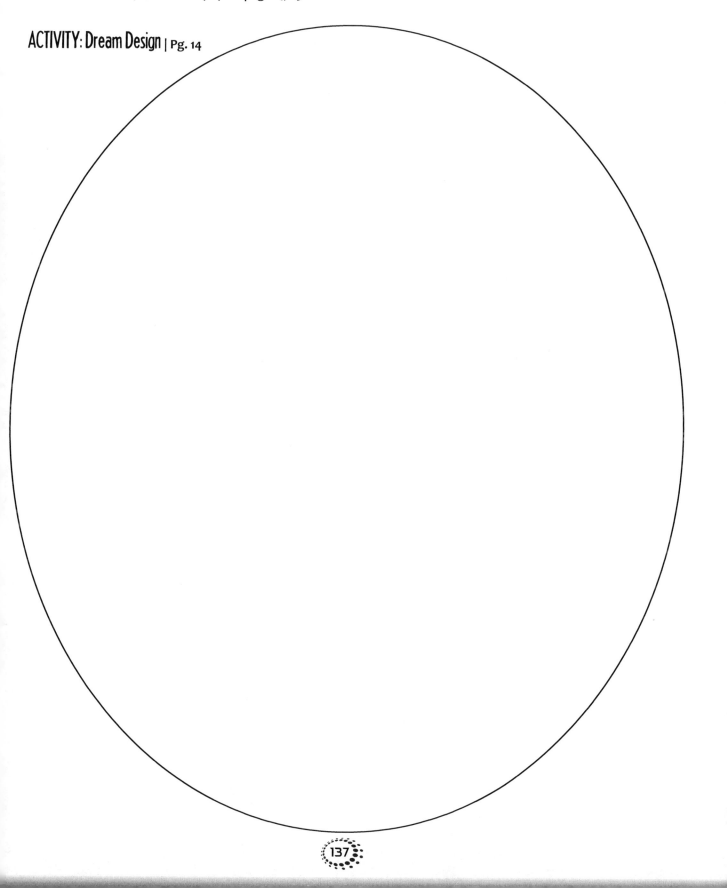

Open Reflection | Pg. 11

Everyday Magnificent | Date: _____

Practice: Energy Medicine Bundle | Pg. 18, 19
Touchstone: Pause-Surrender, Flood Gratitude | Pg. 22, 23

ACTIVITY: Gratitude and Synchronicity | Pg. 10

ACTIVITY: To Be List | Pg. 11

Open Reflection | Pg. 11

Everyday Magnificent | Date: _____

Practice: Intentional Breathing and Unity Coherence | Pg. 16
Touchstone: Jump for Joy and Authentic Movement | Pg. 24

ACTIVITY: Distillation | Pg. 11

Open Reflection | Pg. 11

Practice: Nature Sit | Pg. 18, 21
Touchstone: Flood the Yes | Pg. 22

ACTIVITY: Free Write, Inquiry Prompt: | Pg. 10
Where in my life can I embrace infinite possibilities and stretch outside my comfort zones? Where and how can I take more creative risks in my life?

Open Reflection | Pg. 11

Everyday Magnificent | Date: _____

Practice: Make Music and Vocalize-Tone-Chant-Sing | Pg. 17, 18
Touchstone: Flood Gratitude | Pg. 23

ACTIVITY: Mandala Series | Pg. 12

Open Reflection | Pg. 11

Practice: Intentional Breathing with Seated or Walking Meditation | Pg. 15, 16
Touchstone: Circulate-Radiate | Pg. 22

ACTIVITY: Free Write, Inquiry Prompt: | Pg. 10
Which Everyday Magnificent tools have most impacted my life? How has my life been benefited, and/or my world-view changed since I began this journey?

Everyday Magnificent I Date: _____

Open Reflection | Pg. 11

Everyday Magnificent | Date: _____

Practice: Dancing Meditation | Pg. 17
Touchstone: Sacred Interruptions | Pg. 25

ACTIVITY: Distillation | Pg. 11

Everyday Magnificent | Date: _____

Write a mission statement. Moving forward, what is my commitment to live an Everyday Magnificent life?

Afterwards

I am smiling as I write this because if you engaged earnestly in this process, your rewards now far exceed your efforts. Congratulations for showing up. This journal is complete, though the journey is eternal.

You have written and illustrated a sacred scripture of your deepening relationship with your unlimited nature. This book is charged with wisdom, energy and remembrance. You have documented a model for transformation and used it to flower from the inside out.

I am grateful for how you used this journal as a template to unfold into new possibilities. It's my prayer that it has served your activating a more unlimited life.

I am grateful that you have made it your own. As you move on freely, I intend you replicate and evolve any version of these experiences to continue to shape your reality.

This was just a season, yet enough to integrate new ways of being, creating and relating. Now you are tasked with carrying the practices into the living meditation that is Everyday Magnificent.This is a lifestyle that prioritizes embodiment of our whole being intelligence, in daily, practical, transformative ways.

As we explore our infinite potential, it elevates our lives and ripples out to the world. I practiced and played with most of these tools for decades. I continue to hybridize and reinvent new versions of them - and myself. I notice that when I practice, my soul bubbles joyfully along. I notice I am more curious, grateful, lit up and surrendered to the Mystery of life, as it lives me.

May we value and choose aliveness. May we keep nourishing our love affair with the Unknown and surrendering into the unique ways the Mystery lives through us. May our waking, walking wisdom serve all life.

May we keep creating, and modeling our best selves. May we lose ourselves in the Quantum Field and find our magnificence in and as vast Love, over and over again.

Our living and loving shapes the world.
I wonder how it will all unfold for us?
I cast all my votes for Magnificent!

Evolutionary Love,
Gabriela Masala
www.gabrielamasala.com

Printed and bound by PG in the USA